FLY LOW! FLY HIGH! AIRPLANES OF THE WORLD CHILDREN'S AERONAUTICS & ASTRONAUTICS BOOKS

BABY PROFESSOR

EDUCATION KIDS

Speedy Publishing LLC
40 E. Main St. #1156
Newark, DE 19711
www.speedypublishing.com

All About Airplanes!

Since the early times, people watched birds and wished they could fly.

But birds have hollow bones and feathers that help them to fly.

But with the invention of kites, scientists understood how wind works.

Many people experimented with flight.

The Wright Brothers were successful in building the first airplane.

Orville and Wilbur Wright were the first ones to create the flying machine on December 17, 1903.

The first plane took its first flight for twelve seconds.

From that
day onwards,
inventors
kept on
designing
new kinds
of planes.

During World War I, war planes were built by the government for fighting.

Then commercial airplanes were built to carry people and for cargo transportation.

Engines help the airplanes fly, they provide the thrust needed to move a plane forward.

Thrust is a force that makes the airplane move through the air.

The long body of an airplane is usually called "fuselage".

Pilots control the airplane from a cockpit. Cockpits are located at the front of the fuselage.

Planes have airfoil shaped wings. They help to overcome the effect of gravity.

Airfoil shaped wings makes the air flows faster at the top than the bottom. Air pressure then pushes the airplane up.

Some airplanes are capable of traveling faster than the speed of sound. They are commonly used by the military.

Did you enjoy reading about airplanes? Share this to your friends.

Made in the USA
Las Vegas, NV
10 December 2023

82435236R00026